AWOL in Saigon, Vietnam

The True Story of a Soldier

ROBERT L. RICE

authorHOUSE®

AuthorHouse™
1663 Liberty Drive
Bloomington, IN 47403
www.authorhouse.com
Phone: 1 (800) 839-8640

Published by AuthorHouse 06/24/2015

ISBN: 978-1-5049-1936-4 (sc)
ISBN: 978-1-5049-1937-1 (hc)
ISBN: 978-1-5049-1935-7 (e)

Library of Congress Control Number: 2015910170

Print information available on the last page.

This book is printed on acid-free paper.

Scripture quotations are from the Holy Bible, King James Version
(Authorized Version). First published in 1611. Quoted from the KJV Classic
Reference Bible, copyright © 1983 by the Zondervan Corporation.

To my wife, Frances B. Rice, who has encouraged and supported me throughout this work. Also to our children DeHaviland, Robert L. Jr. (Bobby), Edward, Mirriam, Jermaine, Jammaal, and Cecil.

Contents

Foreword

There were times I didn't think I'd make it back home. At that time, I didn't realize that I was not in charge of my destiny or that God had plans for me. He put His arms of protection around me and brought me safely home, and for that I am grateful.

AWOL in Saigon, Vietnam depicts my life before, during, and after my tour of duty in Vietnam. It took three years for me to complete a twelve-month assignment. You are probably wondering what happened. Well, after being on the battlefield for a short time, I was shot in the left hip, and the bullet exited my left buttock, destroying most of the tissue. I was hospitalized for one and a half months. I had a difficult time trying to walk. The attending physician said I would be on light duty after my stay in the hospital. When I returned to my company, I turned in my medical records with the papers documenting my physical limitations inside the medical record folder. To my surprise, I was told a few days later that I would be returning to the field without limitations. I informed the officer that the doctor's orders stated, "No long standing or prolonged walking." I returned to field duty without limitations as I was instructed, but I was unable to maintain the pace of my company. After a long day of walking and struggling to keep up, my wound reopened. The chopper arrived to pick up the dead and the wounded, and I crawled onto the helicopter and was carried back to the 93rd E-VAC hospital in Long Binh, where my wound was restitched. After I was released, I went to Saigon and partied for a few days. Saigon was about thirty miles from the Long Binh Hospital. When I returned to my unit, I was considered to have been AWOL (absent without leave).

1

How It All Began

I met Frances in Chattanooga, Tennessee, in 1957, when my family moved next door to her family. For me, it was love at first sight. In the months following I tried to get Frances to become my girlfriend but to no avail. I felt belittled because she did not respond to me the way I thought she should have. At that time, I had very low self-esteem because I was already three years behind in school. In the first grade, I had become very ill with asthma and pneumonia. I couldn't go to school, and that created a real problem—and a complex—for me. Because I had had to repeat three grades, other students would make fun of me, which only added to my low self-esteem, coupled with my being overweight. Before I met Frances, the neighborhood children would call me Fat Daddy. I resented being called that name.

Those were the kinds of obstacles that caused me to feel inferior, even though I had friends and girlfriends and was well liked.

At the age of twelve I was a Boy Scout and went to camp for a week. At the time I couldn't swim well enough to be called a swimmer. The day I arrived at camp, the swim instructor asked all scouts who could swim to stand in one line and all non swimmers to stand in another line. Most of my friends got in the swimmers line, and I didn't want to be outdone, so I joined the swimmers line with them. The instructor took all the swimmers down to the lake to be tested. One by one, we had to swim behind a boat for about fifty yards out and back. It was my turn. My only thought was that I had lied. I could swim, but I couldn't swim fifty yards. My plan was to swim out so far and catch the end of the boat. I swam as far as I could, but when I tried to catch the tail end of the boat, I couldn't hold on. Every time I attempted to catch the end of the boat, the instructor would paddle away. He actually thought I was swimming and didn't know I was in trouble. I was ashamed for lying, and I had too much pride to ask for help. I began to drown.

I stopped trying to swim to the boat. I was breathing out my life when the thought occurred that I could never have Frances as a girlfriend. I felt useless, and I asked myself, *Why go on living?* I looked down and saw darkness; I looked up and saw light. The air flowed out of my lungs, and it didn't hurt. I was sinking into death because I felt I was a loser. I did not have the self-confidence to believe I could become a happy person. Then I heard the voice of an angel say, "Get up."

Instantly I came out of the water and grabbed the boat. What seemed like ten minutes was only a few seconds, and no one really knew that I was in trouble. I learned to swim that week at camp, but I almost lost my life in the process. The angel I heard from at camp appeared to me again while I was in Vietnam.

When I was twelve, Frances's brother and I developed a friendship. I attended church with him, and we played together daily. I had joined the church against my mother's wishes. There was an overseer in the church who gave strict orders that the members could only date within the church. The members could not participate in dances, parties, social gatherings, or any after-school activities. The membership could only go to church, school, and work. There was absolutely no participation in any extracurricular activities such as movies or bowling.

The pastor, at that time, was a woman who had no voice. I didn't care that there was no outside entertainment as long as I could be with Frances. I was in love and knew I wanted Frances in my life forever. I grew to love the membership like a real church family, and that was one of the happiest times of my life. At the age of fifteen, I was told that I was a preacher. I later learned that the church was a "cult." It was definitely not like the Baptist Church I attended. The overseer of the church ruled every member's life. She presented herself as the mediator between the members and God. If you were planning a trip, you had to have her permission. She would supposedly consult with God and then give you an answer. If she said no to your request, you had better not go because you would be declared out of the Will of God. Needless to say, we no longer attend that church. Foolish as it may seem, you would actually be amazed how many people would not do things they really wanted to do or go places they really wanted to go without her permission. That church exists today under different leadership and a different set of rules and guidelines.

My sister and I were brought up in a middle-class family environment. We were very happy, even though we didn't have a lot of extras. Both of our parents worked, and they provided for us adequately. We always had everything we needed and some of what we wanted.

As time went on and being around Frances and her family we started dating, Frances and I were first married on May 23, 1964. We did not have a honeymoon. She was sixteen, and I was seventeen. The officials of the church made all the arrangements. My mother did not know about the marriage until after it had taken place. Frances's mother knew about the arrangements since she was a member of the congregation. Frances and I loved each other, but we were not ready for marriage. She was determined to complete high school. I cared about school too, but I cared more about Frances.

I dropped out of school and started working. We lived with Frances's mother. We wanted our own place but couldn't afford it because of our limited income. I thought about going into the army because there I could finish school and learn a trade. When I got out of the army, I would be skilled enough to get a better job and buy a house using the GI Bill.

2

Basic Training

I joined the US Army at the age of seventeen. Frances and I had been married only a few months when I asked my father to sign me into the service against my mother's wishes. As I took the oath, I knew I had made a big mistake. I had to leave the one I loved. I would have to pay for my actions. In boot camp, I was one of the fattest guys in my outfit. I always got the toughest training because I was fat. I did not see the need for extra training but my sergeant did, so he stayed on me. While we were standing in formation, the sergeant called out, "Where is Rice?" "Up, Sarge," I'd answered. He asked, "Did you understand my command?" "Yes, sir," I'd answered.

"Well, since you understood, drop down and give me thirty push-ups." I felt like the sergeant was picking on me. I didn't realize that he was really making me strong and teaching me to believe in myself. When I began basic training, I could only do two correct push-ups. When I completed training, I could do sixty, thanks to my drill sergeant.

Every morning we did a four-mile run. My drill sergeant would run beside me and ask whether I wanted him to stop the entire company for a few minutes so I could get my breath. Well, I was no more tired than anyone else. I was doing fine; in fact, I enjoyed the run.

So my response to him was, "Thanks, but no thanks." The sergeant told me to drop out of the ranks while the other troopers continued to run. He had me do thirty push-ups and then catch up with the company. I did just that. I was proud of myself because I had lost weight, trimmed down, and was looking good.

I learned some life lessons from Sarge. At the time, I thought he was picking on me. During a training event, he caught me with my hands in my pockets. We were not allowed to have our hands in our pockets. He made me empty both of my pockets and give him my personal belongings. I had to fill all my pockets with sand—even my field jacket pockets, which held a lot of sand. Carrying that sand made for an extremely tiresome day. I learned a valuable lesson, which was to do what you are told, and get it right the first time. The service was very beneficial to me. Prior to going into the service, I was inactive. I didn't play sports in school and was considered to be overweight, but by the end of basic training and AIT (Airborne Infantry Training), I was a fit soldier. In addition to being able to do fifty or sixty push-ups, I could run five or six miles nonstop. I was proud of my training.

While training to fire the M-14 rifle, I was observed holding it incorrectly. My sergeant ordered the entire company to stop firing. He asked me, "Why do you have your head up your ass?" He told me to tell the sergeant overseeing our company in a tower about a hundred yards away that I had my head up my ass. When I started to yell out to the sergeant in the tower, my drill sergeant said to me, "No, not yet." He instructed the rest of the company to start firing their weapons and then turned to me and said, "Now tell him." There I stood with over thirty troopers firing their weapons, and I was trying to tell the sergeant in the tower about the position of my head. Needless to say, I made the third-highest score on the M-14 rifle training. I received a three-day pass to go home because of the high score.

Because I had little travel experience, I didn't realize that taking the bus would decrease the time I could spend with my family. I learned a real lesson in travel. The next time I would fly. When Frances saw me, she was shocked that I had lost thirty pounds in two months. She cried because she thought I had been mistreated, but she was proud of my weight loss.

I enjoyed my time at home. I saw my family, my church family, and my friends. While at church, I was told that the church overseer didn't approve of me going to the military. She wanted me to stay home and be a minister at the church.

Because this church was a cult, the overseer did not want ministers to have outside schooling or proper training. I wanted to serve in the military so I could see and experience the outside world. I wanted to complete high school and become a minister and create a financially better life for me and my wife.

At the end of my AIT in Fort Gordon, Georgia, I was assigned to Fort Reilly, Kansas, for my duty station which was First Division, Twenty-Sixth Infantry. Since the church didn't believe in killing, I chose to be a chaplain's assistant.

I thought that once I completed my military duty and became a chaplain's assistant, I would be a full-fledged minister. I did not know the necessary steps it took to become a minister. I informed the military that I was a conscientious objector and that I was willing to do all I could in the service but that I was not willing to kill anyone. I was transferred to the Fifth Army Division Fire Fighting Unit on the airstrip at Fort Riley. We worked twenty-four hours on the job and twenty-four hours off the job. A very relaxed position. During the On Job Training (OJT), I was taught to put out fires, put foam on runways to prepare the runway for airplanes landing on their bellies without landing gear. It was a rewarding experience. I was called a plug man. I made sure water was supplied from the fire hydrant to the fire truck.

While I was working as a fireman, First Division (approximately five thousand men) was deployed to Vietnam. I was with the Fifth Army at that time. I saw the troops on the airfield as I stood with the fire truck. First Division was prepared to depart to Vietnam. Wives and children were crying because their husband and fathers were going off to war. They flew out of Fort Reilly to meet a ship for their journey to Vietnam. The day First

Division departed Fort Riley, the base resembled a ghost town. Only a few bars were open off base, and downtown was empty, because that was an army town.

Three or four months later, I got orders to go to Vietnam. I was given shots and paperwork before I cleared post. They gave me fifteen days of leave time and five days travel time before my departure to Vietnam. I used nineteen days leave time and one day travel time. I had learned from my previous travel experience. I went home to visit my family and my church family. While there, I went hunting with some church brothers, one of whom showed an interest in my wife. While hunting, I missed the targets several times and jokingly told them to pray that I returned home. The brother who showed interest in my wife said, "It doesn't matter how much we pray. If it is meant for you to be killed, then you will be killed." I thought that was a thoughtless thing to say to someone on his way to Vietnam.

My wife was sad; she didn't want to see me leave. She acted a bit indifferent. She was withdrawn and very sorrowful, and I could understand, but I also thought she should be happy to make the most of the time we had together before I was shipped out to Vietnam.

3

Arriving in Vietnam

I checked myself in at the nearest military base so that I would not be AWOL. That Air Force base was between Chattanooga, Tennessee, and Nashville, Tennessee. They put me on a C-130 to Oakland Air Force Base. I traveled from Oakland Air Force Base on a C-141 cargo plane where everyone was seated facing the tail of the plane. We flew to Guam and from Guam into Tan Son Nhut Air Force Base in Saigon, Vietnam. I left the States on the morning of December 24, 1965. After more than twelve hours in the air and crossing the international date line, I missed Christmas Day, arriving in Saigon on December 26, 1965. I had come from a cold climate to an extremely hot tropical climate, and it was a nightmare. When the cabin door of the plane opened, the heat and humidity almost took my breath. I felt certain I wouldn't survive that country, but I learned to adjust.

We stayed at a place called 90th's Replacement. At that time it was located on Tan Son Nhu't. It eventually moved to Long Binh. The odor at Tan Son Nhu't was horrible.

I wasn't used to the odor of the country yet. Female Vietnamese workers in the mess hall or eating area wore what appeared to be black pajamas and funny-looking hats that shielded them from the sun. Their teeth were black or red—not white, as I was accustomed to seeing. Their teeth became this color from chewing betel nut leaves. It was a narcotic that preserved their teeth. The color of their teeth reminded me of the teeth of elderly women in the states who dipped snuff, which stained their teeth a brown color. They smiled as they passed out eating utensils, and that turned my stomach. The first three days I couldn't eat. Hunger pains soon helped me get over the odors and appearances. I went into the mess hall, smiled at mama san, the name given the elderly women of Vietnam, accepted silverware, and ate without a problem.

Several guys there were in transition. They were either going to another base camp or were going home. They informed us of the horror we could expect to see in the fields, including the number of guys that had been killed. I didn't know what to expect. Vietnam was like a dream. It was unreal. I couldn't believe that I was actually in a war situation. It was calm at Saigon Tan Son Nhu't Air Force Base. It housed both Army and Air Force units.

You could not hear bombs or big guns; there was no obvious action.

At 90th Replacement the barracks had electricity and lights. You could take a warm shower. My next duty station would be different. From 90th Replacement some of us were sent to a place called Phouc Vinh, the Big Red One. I was put back in the First Division. It was different from 90th Replacement. We stayed in tents without electricity or hot showers. The floor was ground grass and mud. The mosquitoes were as big as flies. Thousands would come out at the same time every night and buzz until three o'clock in the morning when they departed as if someone had called them home.

There were fifteen guys to a tent. We took showers outside the tent, where there was an overhead fixture with a bag of water held together with three poles. The sun heated the water bag, and the water would trickle down, providing a warm shower. This was the basic camp where our belongings stayed while we fought in the field. I met guys I was going to be with for the next twelve months. The ones who had been there for a while told us new arrivals to stay around them, and they would take care of us.

The first guy I met was an American from the Philippines. We became friends right away. He had arrived in Vietnam a few days ahead of me. Several of the guys tried to escape the horror of losing a friend in combat by not becoming friends with anyone. But it was hard to remain alone or try not to like someone just because you thought you might lose them. It was a chance we all took.

I don't remember my friend's name, but he and I pulled guard duty together. We talked about our families while in a bunker on the perimeter of base camp. He always talked so affectionately about his wife and kids. I could picture his family life.

Beyond the bunkers, the trees were cut low so that we could see beyond them. Land mines were set up in case the enemy got inside the perimeter. That was our protection. If by chance they slipped inside the perimeter without our knowledge, we would be warned because they would be blown up before they got to the bunker where we were. Concertina wires and booby traps were also part of our protection.

There was a safety lane—a straight pathway—that allowed us to walk beyond the perimeter. We had to know exactly where that pathway was because it was no more than two feet wide. It was wide enough for one guy to walk through and get past all the land mines and booby traps without stepping on one and blowing up himself and others around him.

In the bunker, my friend and I sat and talked about our families and shared our pictures. We got to know each other quite well. It was totally dark in our basic camp on Phouc Vinh, so we had to use flashlights or cigarette lighters. In our tents we used candles because there was no electricity.

One night while sitting around the foot locker with a candle burning in the midst, we smoked pot. That was my first time smoking marijuana. I had never felt like that before, and I started tripping. I looked at one of the guys in the tent, and it appeared that some of his teeth were missing. I started laughing at him and could not stop. I could also see the light of the candle illuminating my arm. I was so scared; yet, still laughing, I ran out into the night air and looked up at the stars and said, "I will never smoke that stuff again." I lied.

While on guard duty and smoking, we sat and gazed out of the bunker at tree stumps that appeared to be moving toward us. I shot one of the tree stumps, but it kept moving. Marijuana, like any other drug, messes with your mind, hampering your ability to think and make wise decisions. We called to Rear Area and warned them that there was movement.

There was no movement, but we were so afraid and didn't know what to expect. This was our third week in Vietnam, and we thought it was the enemy walking inside the perimeter. We shot at many tree stumps. The head command bunker asked what we were shooting. We told him we thought we had movement. They checked and informed us there was no movement; only tree stumps out there. It was comical at times. We continued smoking marijuana; that's what distorted our vision. Inside the bunkers after a rain, it was muddy, dirty, and nasty, but we learned to live with those conditions. That was my initial introduction to the front line. It was not so bad, since we only killed a few tree stumps.

Finally, we started going on search-and-destroy missions. We walked all day. That was called sweeping an area—making sure it was free of VC or Viet Cong. When we ran into the VC, we engaged them in a firefight. My initial realization that we were in a war was when an NBC cameraman started to film the action and then suddenly slumped over. He had been shot.

The jungle was so thick you could not see the enemies you shot.

After a battle we would see blood but no bodies. That was called psychological warfare. The enemies hid their dead and wounded from us to try to distort our minds. They wanted us to believe that we had used a lot of firepower but had not killed anyone. They aimed at playing with our minds. After that battle, I knew we were not engaged in a maneuvers or training. It really hit me that we were in combat and that this was the real thing. All that I had learned in basic and combat training had begun to pay off. From that point on, I got a little cold. That is, numb to death, killing, and fighting. I did not care what happened; my goal was to live. I became obsessed with killing. I forgot about my ministry of sparing a life. I was tired of seeing my friends killed or blown up by landmines.

I became a firefighting team leader. I had an M-14 E2AR, which had a tripod. In my sector, there was a guy who was an M-60 machine gunner, others who had M-14s, and there was Joe, who was an M-79 gunner. I was the leader of a six-man team. We patrolled the left flank or the right flank of the company in sweeping.

JJ, one of the guys on the fire team, and I formed a close bond. Sergeant Payne was over our team. Our team was together until I got shot. Whenever there were maneuvers or we were on a listening post, we talked about what happened back in the States, which we sometimes called the world.

On one occasion, Sergeant Payne and I were sitting around talking about Moms Mabely, an adult party recorder. After walking all day with no contact with the enemy, we dug our foxhole for the night. I took my shoes off so my feet could get some air. Sergeant Payne and I were sitting side by side on the pile of dirt we had just dug when suddenly a tracer round came between us. When a tracer bullet is fired from a gun, it illuminates. Hurriedly, I put my shoes on, and we fought the enemy for the rest of the night.

A listening post was set up when forty to sixty guys or more were in the field. While the company of troops slept, five or six guys set up patrol on all four flanks of the company. We would set up so many feet on all four sides of the company to warn them if contact was made by the approaching enemy. That would give the company time to wake up and prepare for a fight.

One night during the raining season five of us were on a listening patrol or LP. It was 12:00 a.m., and it was my time to stay up and watch for two hours. We all took turns staying up for one or two hours. It was quite peaceful as I waited for something to happen. Since it was still raining, I covered my head with my poncho and smoked a cigarette while the other four guys slept. I sat, content, looking down a path illuminated by the light of the moon. The enemy was somewhere out there waiting, just as I was waiting. The rain provided a tranquil state of mind in the midst of danger. I always feel at peace when it rains. At that time I did not know that I snored, and when it was my turn to sleep, Sergeant Payne would wake me and say, "Rice, wake up! You're giving our position away." I would tell him okay and go back to sleep, and he would wake me again and whisper, "Rice, you're snoring."

I have been asked since returning stateside, "How could you sleep in a combat zone?"

I always say that when the body is tired, and you get a break, you will sleep. I would lay my head back in my steel pot (helmet) and dream that I was anywhere but Vietnam. After Sergeant Payne woke me, we would go back and forth, arguing about my snoring. When we returned to basic camp, he would tell the other guys, "Don't take Rice on patrol because he snores too loud. He will give your position away."

Years later, after returning to the States, I was in my bed asleep and heard myself snoring. I laughed and thought about Sergeant Payne and how I had argued with him.

We were in the field for weeks at a time without a baths. We sometimes used our helmets to hold water for sponge baths or to shave. We did not wear underclothes because we did not have the time or the place to take baths or keep our clothes clean. In the field we were dirty, always wading in muddy water. I had dirt under my fingernails and cuts on my arms and hands that I thought would never heal All of us had a pungent odor that could be smelled miles away.

In some of the battles, I saw people blown apart. Some of the enemies had holes in their bodies. The sun baked them, and they were swollen, and there remained the smell of death. Bodies decayed in the tropical heat. The smell is one I'll never forget.

During Operation Crimp, which was featured in *Newsweek* magazine, we found tunnels that were two miles long.

and he finally agreed to let us move our position, but it was too late. By that time, the enemy had discovered us. They started shooting at us, and we shot back. We were in a battle. Tim positioned that M-79 and started dropping projectiles directly on the VC.

It was a beautiful sight to see him handle that weapon so well. It was night, but we could see by the light of fire that the VC had made. Tim was smiling as he fought with all his might. We killed all of them, and we did not lose a single man that night. The remainder of the night was quiet and still.

We pushed our way into the L-shaped ambush. They lay down such powerful firepower that we had to take cover. I took cover behind an ant hill. I looked over and saw my company commander and his radio man take cover behind another ant mound. He called out, "Charge! Charge!" I got up to advance, and one of two things happened. Either a single projectile round hit my weapon, breaking it in half and striking me in the hip and exiting my left buttock, or more than one bullet hit me and my weapon. Being shot was like being tackled playing football. I was hit in the hip and knocked senseless. Upon impact, everything instantly went into slow motion, and I was dazed from the time I was shot until I hit the ground. That took only seconds but seemed like five minutes. As I was falling to the ground, I thought to myself that I needed to get to the ground in a hurry before another bullet hit me in the head or chest. When I hit the ground, everything came into focus. I immediately rolled over on my side, but I couldn't move my left leg because it was numb. My first thought was that my leg had been severed. I felt vulnerable and helpless, and I couldn't use my weapon to protect myself if I was approached by the enemy. I couldn't move, so there was nothing to do but wait for help. Sarge was about twenty-five feet away from me, and he asked if I was all right. I said, "Yes, I've been hit, man." They continued to fight and tried to cover me and others, and our company commander shouted, "Charge!" The medic arrived on the scene. He cut through my trousers and exposed my rear end. He said, "Rice, you just shot in the ass, man. You'll be all right." I didn't know where I was shot. I just knew I was shot and numb on my left side from the waist down. He patched my wound and gave me morphine.

I continued bleeding from the hip area, but, due to the excitement, that wound was not detected. By that time, the pain was unbearable. Later I asked another medic for more medication. He gave me another shot of morphine. Someone gave me a .45 hand gun with which to defend myself. The VC continued shooting at me while I waited to for someone to move me to a safer area.

The wounded and dead were scattered across the field, lying where they were shot or killed. I lay there naked from the waist down while the battle continued. The company commander ordered the company to charge the enemy's bunker. The Viet Cong never stopped shooting at me. The dirt in front of me popped up where the bullets struck the ground. I looked up, but I didn't see the enemy, so I lay still. I could hear the wounded guys calling for help. Young men from nineteen years to twenty-five years of age were calling on the Lord and for their mothers. Everybody called on the Lord for help, even those who said they didn't believe in Him. I was so miserable I prayed and asked God to take me. I was ready to die, especially when I saw a soldier shot in the head crawling on the ground with half his face hanging off his head calling for his mother. I needed to get out of that situation. It was like playing bid wiz card game. I wanted to go out the back door of life since I couldn't come in the front door. I had lost the will to live. Ninety percent of living is in the mind. When one loses the will to live, death is near.

I lay in grass a foot tall. I felt that I would be shot at any time. I could shoot back, but I couldn't stand or walk. I was still bleeding; again, I asked the Lord to take me. *Please, just let me die.* I had made my peace with the Lord and was ready to go to heaven. I have experienced some real highs in my life with marijuana and some of Vietnam's best opium. I'd gotten very drunk and felt pretty good, but I had never experienced peace like I was about to feel.

I was fully conscious when I began to enter into death. There was a peace that came to me, and I wanted to go wherever it was taking me. I knew I was dying.

The sound of the war activity ceased. I could barely hear the shooting or the wounded soldiers crying out around me. I had no pain. I could see the battlefield but was detached from the battle as though I was not a part of it.

As I lay there waiting to die, a man appeared sitting on a rock. He wasn't in the battle but sat nearby talking to me. That man had a book in his hand and appeared to be reading. His clothes were the kind that would not get dirty. He wore a sparkling white robe. I could see through this man. When he talked, he did not move his mouth but I heard him in my mind, and I talked to him the same way. I communicated without moving my lips. Seemingly, his job was to convince me to live.

I later realized (some twenty-two years later, after I was back home in church) that an angel had visited me. According to the Holy Bible (Hebrews 1:14), *Angels are ministering spirits.*[1] The angel visited me and reasoned with me as to why I should live. The angel asked me about my mother, father, sisters, and brother.

He reminded me of the good times I had at home. Until now I had not thought about my family. I love my family, but I wanted more of this peace I was feeling. I wanted to die. Then he asked, "What about your wife"? That was the first time I had thought about my wife.

I said, "Oh, I love my wife, and I don't want to leave her." The angel knew that the only thing that would make me want to cling to life was the love of my wife. When I told him I didn't want to leave my wife, the angel said I was not going to die. It was not my time to die. After the angel assured me that I wasn't going to die, that in fact I had to live through this hell, he left me. After he left, the pain returned, along with the loud sound of crying soldiers, the agony, and the sounds of shooting guns. And the feeling of coldness returned to my body. I continued to lose blood, but I knew I would live. I cursed because I realized I was going to have to live through this ordeal. By this time, Sarge came to me and said, "Rice, they're shooting at us, and we have to get you out of here."

I had had two shots of morphine and was still hurting like hell. Sarge put his weapon across my legs as we both lay on the ground. The enemy was still shooting at us. He then put my bad leg over my good leg and pulled me. He told me to push. When I pushed away, I saw a big puddle of blood that had drained from my body. *I left my blood on the battlefield that day.*

I deserve all the rights a veteran should have because I fought that war with all I had to offer and almost died, as so many others did.

It seemed like an eternity before we got to a safe area. Sarge asked how was I doing, and I told him I was hurting like hell. When the medic made his rounds to check up on me, I asked for more pain medication, but he said he could not give me any more; I had had too much already. I begged for more; the pain felt like air was flowing through the holes in my body. Finally he gave me another shot of morphine, but it didn't faze the pain.

Our guys picked up the wounded and the dead, putting us all on the same truck to get us out of the hostile area as soon as possible. The battle was still raging, and although we were not in the thick of the fighting, we were still close enough for the bullet rounds to come our way.

Tim was up front with the driver talking crazy. He said he was going back to get the one who shot me. He had been shot in the arm, and maybe the morphine affected his thinking. I did not see him after that ride to the outpost field hospital.

They threw my friend from the Philippine on the back of the truck with the rest of us, dead and wounded. The guys said to me when they threw him onto the truck, "He's dead," but I didn't want to believe them. He landed on his back, his steel pot still on his head, and as the truck moved, his eyes came open, and I tried to talk to him, but he was dead. To this day I will never forget him.

While waiting to be taken to the field hospital, I asked some guys who were smoking weed for a hit of the marijuana they were smoking, and the weed, along with the morphine, made the pain tolerable.

Try to understand: I was nineteen years old; I had on no underwear, and my ass was up in the air; my body was in pain; and my friends were dying, but I was still here. We traveled to a field hospital where doctors sorted out the wounded by their condition. The critically wounded were set aside to die; others were treated and put on choppers to go to a larger hospital—93rd E-VAC at Long Binh. Some of the ones who were left to die did live to make the trip to the hospital and did not end up in body bags.

I was shot around 4:00 p.m., but I didn't get to 93rd E-VAC hospital until 8:00 p.m. I never lost consciousness. I was awake the entire time, even though I was highly drugged. It was at the field hospital that a doctor discovered I had been shot in the hip. The doctor said, "This man has been shot in the hip. Didn't anybody know that?" I didn't know it, either. I only knew that I was in pain and was very cold. In Vietnam it would get to be 110 degrees. I was shivering cold, high and full of morphine, but still in pain. The doctors patched me up and put me on a chopper with other wounded men. They took us to 93rd E-VAC in Long Binh. It was the largest hospital facility that I knew about down south. While we were traveling to the hospital, the vibration from the chopper blade greatly intensified the pain. It was dark when we got to the hospital. It reminded me of the TV series *M*A*S*H*.

The orderlies got us off the chopper. When they attempted to transport me from the cot to the operating bed, they lifted my legs, and gravity pulled the wound down. The pain was so severe, I told them I'd get myself onto the bed.

After shifting about, I finally made it to the bed that I was on when I was carried into the operating room. The operating room was unlike those you see in the States.

It was inside a tent with flesh and blood on the floor. Workers cleaned the floor as quickly as possible.

Doctors worked on guys and cut out burned flesh that was contaminated. Blood and flesh was everywhere. The doctor instructed me to lie still on my side in a fetal position. He promised to stop my pain.

He gave me a spinal tap. As he released the fluid into my spin, it felt like ice entering my body. The pain was blocked from my chest down. I had no feeling; the pain had stopped. The only way I could tell I was being moved or treated was by the moving of my head. I was high from all the morphine I was given in the field, and what the doctors gave me at the field hospital only made me higher. A guy named Don had been shot in the thigh, and the bullet had exited his upper back. He was unconscious on the operating table. I looked over and saw them working on him. He had a large gash in his leg.

They cleaned his wound and waited a few days to be sure no infection set in before they stitched the wound. They did me the same way. I drained for five days before I was stitched. After they finished with me in the operating room, they took me to a ward. I didn't sleep that night. It was the next day before I went to sleep. Although they changed the bandages on a regular basis, I stayed wet for a week. It was miserable being in that condition for five days. After the fifth day, I was taken back to the operating room, and they put me to sleep while my wound was stitched.

This entire time I never used the bathroom to have a bowel movement. In fact, I don't think I used the bathroom to have a bowel movement for about two weeks. I could hardly walk, for one thing, and they were only giving me liquids. I was still in semi shock, realizing what I had gone through. Every night I dreamed about shooting at the women along the road. What was disgusting was the women I killed the very day I was wounded. Even today as I sit and write this book, I can still see the women falling from the shots of my weapon. Some guys wanted to count the number they had killed. Not I. I did not want to see their faces.

The day I was wounded we did a sweep and came upon an ant field. During the rainy season, ants built tall houses that stood four to six feet high; they built columns of them. During the dry season, the ant houses were hard as bricks. The Vietnamese women soldiers caught us coming through the ant field and opened fire on us. They pinned us down for a while, but we were able to overrun them. As they ran away, I laid down a field of fire and killed those women. I killed some men, too, but killing the women hurt me the most. It was in my head; I couldn't stop thinking about it. I killed a woman.

A young Vietnamese girl at the hospital came by and cleaned around the beds daily. She talked to me, but I didn't understand her because I did not speak the language. I don't know why she took a liking to me, but I was comforted by her company. She manicured my nails and talked as if I understood her. Listening to her talk, I learned to speak their language. She said to me, "Dia plum," which meant "nice fingernails." My skin was badly scarred from being in the field, and I was dirty because it had been several weeks since I bathed. Scratches covered my hands and arms, but with the care she gave me, I started to look better.

I met others guys while I was in the hospital. One was in my company. He was hurt rather badly while sitting on the back of a jeep that was pulling a trailer full of supplies. The wheel of the jeep hit a land mine that blew up between the jeep and trailer. It tore out all of his stomach area, gutting him from his navel to his chest. It did not damage his face.

The day I was shot I had seen him lying on the ground with other wounded soldiers. He was holding his guts together with gauze while he smoked a cigarette. Another guy I knew was shot in the knee, and he died of shock. It was really strange to see how some died with minor wounds, and others with severe wounds survived. The guy whose intestines were blown out went from being bent over to standing straight and walking. Stitches lined his stomach like buttons. Another guy I knew from basic training was loading or unloading a truck when it jumped out of gear and pinned him against a building, crushing his chest wall. There were several of us who knew each other. The hospital served soldiers from units stationed all over Vietnam.

I became addicted to the medicine I took for pain. I did not know anything about being addicted. I didn't know about drugs until I went into the service. Prior to that time, I had not had a beer, not to mention other kinds of drugs. Every day about thirty minutes before it was time for me to receive the medication, I felt I was having severe pain. It was like clockwork. The orderly told me that I was getting hooked on the drugs. I didn't think I was because I was hurting. I used crutches to assist me when I walked. One day the orderly said to me, "You think you have it bad. You need to go with me." The hospital had four wings; it was made like a cross with an oval-shaped roof. You could look down your wing and see only the nurses' station. The nurse monitored

"Yes, if you don't want it." In the field I ate what I could get. We had C rations or ate the enemy's peanuts after we ran them off. So eating chicken in the stockade was like eating at a famous restaurant. After I was done eating the chicken, the guy that gave it to me came back and told me to be sure to put my underwear on backward that night. I had never been approached like that in my life. I wasn't sure what he meant, but I finally realized that he planned to have sex with me because I had accepted his chicken. In other words, he had bought me for the price of a piece of fried chicken. I knew I would not be putting my underwear on backward.

The guard took me to my tent. There were twenty inmate bunks to a tent; he showed me my bed. The stockade was like a prison camp. It looked like something you saw on TV; high barbed wire fences and saddle port gates at the main entrance. It was a makeshift jail; the inmate housing was made of wood box framing with concrete floors and a large canvas tent draped over the wood frame. It was secured so the wind could not blow the canvas away. Because of the tropical weather, it got very hot. The canvas draped over the sides of the wood frame structure and rolled up with straps so air could circulate through the building. The canvas was let down when it rained. There were twenty four beds/inmates on each side and a long corridor in the middle. There were nine tents in the stockade, along with the mess hall. The administration office and the tower that housed a loud speaker were on the outer part of the stockade. They were adjacent to the sally port or the entrance gate. The fences were doubled with very harmful wire. On all four sides were guard towers, each housing two guards, with M-60s machine guns mounted. I set my mind to do six months in the stockade.

While I was sitting on my bunk, the guy who gave me the chicken walked in. He approached me as if he came to fight or take advantage of me. I thought to myself, *We are in a jail in Vietnam, and he has something like that on his mind.* It was really a power struggle. The real issue was not sex. We slept on cots, and at each end of the cot was a bunk adapter, which was a long piece of wood that kept the cot from collapsing. I kicked the bunk adapter loose and pulled it out. When he realized what I was doing, he leaped over on to me, and I started whaling on his ass with that bunk adapter. He soon realized that I was a fighter and not a pushover. After that night, we became friends. Well, we weren't really friends because I was always careful to feed him from a long-handled spoon. He thought we were friends. After the fight, the guys around me knew that I was a stand-up kind of guy, and that gained me respect from the other inmates.

That was the beginning of my journey in the stockade. I sat and thought about the blood I lost in Vietnam (for my country) and how I almost lost my life, and because I was a few days late returning to my company I was in jail doing time. When confined in the stockade, your military time stops. In other words, twelve months was considered a tour of duty in Vietnam. If you completed six months of duty and were sent to the stockade for six months, you would have six more months to go to make up for the six months you were in the stockade. While in the stockade your pay and time ceases, but you are still in a hostile country.

During the day, we had to go to various outfits on the outskirts of Saigon, the outskirts of Tan Son Nhut' Air Force Base, and other army installations in Saigon, in addition to other places that GIs stayed. That area was considered to be downtown.

Anyone entering the barracks had to pass the guards, who were surrounded by sandbags. As inmates, we had to keep the sandbags filled and maintained to fortify the MPs (military police) entering the compounds where the GIs lived. The GIs who lived downtown and around Saigon did not carry weapons. They worked in air-conditioned offices and had the best of everything, including hot and cold running water. Downtown Saigon was a big metropolitan city. The French had lived there before the Americans occupied Vietnam. Many Vietnamese spoke French and English. The French built and left behind big, elaborate, luxurious mansions, and some French still lived in Vietnam.

Every day we got on trucks that carried us to work sites and brought us back at the end of the day. There were six or seven inmates to a truck, wearing a white armband around the left arm that identified to others that we were prisoners. The prison guard who watched over us had a .12 gauge shotgun, and if we tried to escape, he had the authority to shoot to kill. While we were on the work sites, we were somehow able to buy marijuana and smuggle it back into the stockade. That was our daily routine.

I stayed in jail two and a half months on a six-month sentence. While confined I asked myself, *Why is my country doing this to me? I was the one who was shot; I am the one who's fighting for my country; and because I was late I was charged with being AWOL.* I was only nineteen, and this entire situation was boggling my mind. I just did not understand, and I became a changed person. After that, it was difficult for me to deal with authority figures. I began to think that it was my job to take care of Robert Rice. I could no longer depend on anyone else. I didn't care about anyone's rank or what his position was in the armed forces. After completing two and a half months in the stockade, I got out because of good behavior. The two and a half months gave me time for my wound to heal, and it never came open again. I was released and sent back to my unit in Phouc Vinh, where I went back to the field. My unit continued to do routine sweeping and search-and-destroy missions.

One day after walking what seemed like all day, we came upon a road that was populated by cars—1954 Fords; Buick; a 1949 Chevrolet, and other old cars. It seemed like we had walked back to the United States. The year was 1966, and here were all these old, familiar cars. That was one of the strange incidents that occurred in the fields of Vietnam.

We engaged in firefights with the VC. They would shoot, killing some of us, and run back into the brush into holes that we did not detect until later. We returned fire where we thought the enemies were, but the brush prevented us from seeing them. We realized we had killed some of them when the firefight was over, and we swept the area for casualties and found blood. The VC would move the bodies so we would think that we had done no harm to them. That was called psychological warfare. They tried to play the mind game on us, and sometimes it worked.

There were holes and tunnels that covered the entire areas where we were fighting. There was an occasion when my instinct told me something was about to happen. The VC had chained some of their own men into trees with weapons to attack us when we passed underneath. They had shackled them to a death mission. We saw them in time to kill them before they hit us, and they fell, dangling from the trees with their weapons shackled to their limbs. I saw some terrible things that boggled my mind—things that were foreign to a nineteen-year-old kid who had been reared on apple pie, hot dogs, and cartoons, who was suddenly fighting a war with an enemy who was determined to win at any cost.

There was a strange type of terrain in Vietnam called water table. On one occasion we were down in a rice patch where there was lots of water. I walked onto a spot, and as I stood there, the ground moved in a watery motion. I looked down at the ground it was moving, a two-feet-wide area of ground with water under the ground give you the sensation of break through the ground and fall in the water. On another occasion a chopper was taking our company to a landing zone in the middle of a rice field. The enemy was shooting as we were coming into the LZ (landing zone), and you could hear the rounds hitting the side of the chopper. The gunners on the chopper were literally pushing us off the chopper so they could get away from the enemy's fire. I dropped about ten or fifteen feet and landed in the rice paddy, where I got stuck in the muddy water. The enemy continued shooting at us, but I could not return fire because I couldn't free my right foot. Finally one of the guys came back under fire and got me free, and we got to the edge of the rice paddy, where we took cover. That was a bad feeling.

One day in the bush we run out of C-rations, and we had no food for two days. We survived on the fruit on the trees, in particular, a green and yellow melon the Vietnamese call pomelo. Inside it was a white, sticky, rubbery substance that looked like a big grapefruit. When you opened it with your hands, no juice escaped. Inside there were slices, and each slice contained beads of juice. You could pull a melon down from the tree, and once you cut your way inside, pull out a slice, pop some of the beads in your mouth, and along with some peanuts we got that had been roasting in the sun when we raided a village we came through, and you had a meal. When we came to a village that we thought was supporting the VC, we would burn the houses, kill all the animals, and carry any food we could, like the peanuts that had been baking on a canvas in the sun. They were small but very tasty.

We filled our pockets with those tasty peanuts, and you could hear the peanuts rustling when we walked, but that was no problem with sixty GIs walking through the bush. On one occasion we could not get to the place where the chopper dropped our supplies. It was only maybe ten minutes, if that, but it was long enough for the VC to booby-trap the load, so when our guys tried to retrieve the supplies, they were critically wounded. We would also sometimes run out of water. The weather was hot and humid, and when we walked all day, sweating, our bodies craved water, and we came upon a stream, we were so thirsty and hot, we didn't purify the water before we drank.

The purification tablet were put into canteens full of undrinkable creek water to purify it. But sometimes we could not wait for the purification process to work, and it's a wonder we didn't get really sick from drinking contaminated creek water. We didn't worry about getting sick; if we didn't worry about men killing one another and the horror of combat and field life, then a little bad water was no problem.

As we maneuvered our way upstream one day, we saw a dead water buffalo in the water. None of us were affected by the dead buffalo; quenching our thirst was most important. It seems that living in the field reduces you to an animal.

We were sitting around one day taking a rest from walking, beating the bush chasing the VC, and we were hungry. My stomach was groaning, as some of the guys talked about the type of food their mothers cooked. I thought about what my mother had said to me once. At dinner one night we had beans, fried chicken, cole slaw, corn bread, and lemon pie. I mouthed off, saying, "I'm tired of eating beans." My mother said to me, "One day you will wish you had these beans." It seemed like I could visualize my mother over my head talking, as if to say, "See, I told you so." After that experience of hunger, I learned not to waste food. I thought about how blessed we are in America, where there is a food stand on every corner.

We finally returned to our base camp, where we could let our guard down. Our battalion's base camp was located in Phouc Vinh, where a thousand men or more held down the base. We pulled some guard duty, periodically swept the outer perimeter, rested, cleaned our weapons, and went to the E.M. Club, where we drank beer, played cards, and tried not to think about war.

But that wasn't easy to do with big guns on base, like 105s and 155s, which rang out all night.

For a long time after I returned home, I couldn't sleep without the sounds of the big guns. I slept soundly as long as I could hear the guns. I could tell the difference between guns shooting and rockets and mortar attacks coming into base camp.

The enemy could shoot mortar rounds with such percussion you get the visual of a giant man walking, You could almost tell where the next round would land simply by where the last one hit.

There was a time when I wanted to see my wife. I wanted to travel to Bangkok or the Philippines for a seven-day R&R (rest and recuperation). Many of the guys had gone, but I had not had the opportunity to go on R&R. After a soldier had served six months in Vietnam, the military would pay for a seven-day trip to a place like the Philippines. At this time I had been in Vietnam for eight months, but I had just gotten out of jail in LBJ. I put in a request to go on R&R and was turned down. I was quite upset. I talked to my company commander and expressed to him that I had been in Vietnam for eight months and needed a break. He told me in no uncertain terms that I was not going on R&R, and he ordered me back to the field. I went AWOL. I caught a chopper and went back to Saigon. I met up with a guy I knew in the stockade, who was in the Air Force and stationed in Saigon.

While we were in the stockade, my buddy talked about the good times they had in Saigon near the Air Force base. We never had times like that in the field, where I was stationed. He talked about the nice beds and the hot and cold running water. The lodgings had two people to a room (called cubes). That's the Air Force for you—first class all the way. At the base camp where I was, we all slept in one big hooch.

After I arrived in Saigon, I found my buddy, and we went downtown partying. We were about the same size, since I was thin in those days, so I wore his civilian clothes. He took me to a place called Ken Hoi or Soul City, located across the bridge from downtown Saigon. It was a row of clubs catering to blacks. There were very few whites there because of the music. The Vietnamese girls would say, "Soul brothers No. one." That place had a hometown feel.

I began to notice Vietnamese outside the club whom I suspected were VC. I believed they were the enemy moving supplies on their backs. Ken Hoi is next to the waterfront near the port of Saigon. I told my friend about my suspicion, and he said I was high on weed. But I was also high in the field; I knew a VC when the hair stood up on my back. I was a combat soldier; I had fought the enemy, whereas my friend did not know combat. The VC were very friendly. They stopped and drank or smoked weed with us, and the hair was still standing up on my back. I couldn't understand what they were saying, but they treated us like we belonged with them. They too were dark-skinned. I don't know if it was because of the sun or if that was their natural skin color. Many Vietnamese had dark complexions but were not classified as blacks.

I met several guys from Chattanooga—Duke, Bem, Shaw, and Fred, to name a few. Two of them I met in Saigon, but Fred I knew well, and it was so exciting to see someone from home. Saigon was such a beautiful place. There were shopping centers, theaters where you could see plays and attend shows, and some of the finest restaurants. I fell in love with the city. I was AWOL for three weeks before I returned to base camp, and then I was court-martialed. This was my second special court-martial, and I was given a six-month sentence. This time

I had to complete the entire sentence. I was given credit for good behavior and completed the six-month sentence in five and a half months. By this time the stockade had moved from Tan-Son-Nhut, Saigon, to a place called Long Binh, which was about forty or fifty miles farther north up Highway One. 90th Replacement was located along Highway One, and other side of Highway One about five miles, was an Air Force base called Ben Wau.

Long Binh was on one side of Highway One, and Ben Wau was on the other side. 90th Replacement was located on Long Binh, where there was an ammunition dump and a newly built stockade. That stockade was awesome—and massive, compared to the one at Tan Son Nhut. Tan Son Nhut held about 150 to 200 prisoners, if that many, whereas Long Binh could hold more than 800 men. It had an outer fence and an inner fence that surrounded the stockade, and there was corded razor wire between the two fences and on top of them. There was a third strand of corded razor wire on the ground inside the two fences. It deterred anyone from thinking about escaping. There were also huge towers with M-60 machine guns mounted on all four corners and on the back side of the stockade.

Prisoners were strip-searched at random before entering the stockade after a work detail. The mess hall was directly in front of the saddle port gate where you entered the stockade, and to the left as you entered was the parolee area. Prisoners on this side could go out to a detail unescorted. They did not wear a white arm band. They only displayed an identity badge, and if you did not know, you could not tell whether or not they were prisoners. To the right side of the saddle port gate was maximum security for the white arm band wearers.

Six prisoners were assigned to each armed escort guard, who packed a short-barrel shotgun. He marched his prisoners to work and back to jail. He took the six prisoners on a detail to fill sand bags. As we worked, one guard said, "I've been in Vietnam for three months, and I haven't shot anyone. I sure would like to know what it feels like to shoot someone. Why don't one of you boys run so I can shoot you? I would shoot one of you niggers just like I would a VC." We asked to be taken back to the stockade. We refused to work under a guard like him. We arrived at the stockade and explained what happened. "No big deal" was the attitude. That guard continued working at the stockade, but we were assigned to another guard. We were sent to the sand pit called Big Red.

There we were in Vietnam—prisoners in a war zone. I thought that was so unfair because you could not defend yourself. For a long time we didn't have bunkers or any other place to go if there was a rocket or mortar attack inside the compound. Initially, there was no means of self-protection, but later that issue was corrected. If anyone was killed while in the stockade, military officials told the families that their loved ones were killed in action; in reality they were in the stockade, unable to protect themselves. Seventy percent of those in positions of authority, mainly the guards, used that power to harass the prisoners and make their lives miserable. We were all supposed to be on the same team, but unfortunately some were incarcerated.

There was a maximum security called the Hole, which was designed to drive you crazy or give you a mental whipping. The door to the stall of a single cell had an opening at the bottom which allowed you to see across to the other cell and receive your meals. Each cell had concrete floors and was three feet wide and six to seven feet long. You could see the ceiling, but there was a wire three or four feet from the floor that prevented you from standing. Beyond that wire was a 200-watt light that stayed on at all times. We slept on the concrete floors, clad in our undershorts, and at night we were given a blanket. The first time I went to the Hole, they gave me a Bible and a blanket. When they realized that the soldiers were able to maintain their sanity by reading the Bible, they stopped giving out Bibles. We resulted to doing push-ups to stay sane. Push-ups were a way of tiring yourself out so that you would not go insane. The walls would close in on me when I was in the Hole. I once told the prisoner in the cell next to me that the walls were moving in on me, and he told me to do push-ups until I got tired. It worked. That kept me from crying.

Today I have a problem with elevators and being closed in because of the Hole—or Box, as it was sometimes called. The only clothing allowed was undershorts—no T-shirt. There was a lot of noise—inmates calling out, guards cursing, and periodically you would hear the guards drag an inmate out of his cell and beat him for little or nothing. There were two types of food served in the Hole—regular food and something called DS chow, which consisted of corn flakes, water, raw potatoes, carrots, and bread. DS chow was given to prisoners who gave the guards a hard time, along with other punishments. Sometimes prisoners were put in chains; their feet were chained to their hands, and their hands were chained behind their backs. They had to eat their meals with their mouths like dogs. You were only allowed three bathroom breaks a day. If a prisoner had to go to the bathroom more than three times, and he was a small guy, he got beaten. If he was bigger, it was too much trouble to jump him. We had to take cold showers early in the morning when the water was coldest.

When a soldier is confined after spending a lot of time in the field, he can go into a mental rage or go insane. You have time to think of the people you killed and friends that got killed. That has a grave effect on the mind and can induce mental instability. A prisoner I saw go crazy in the Hole was eating his own feces. The guards were sure he was acting, but when he was let out of his cell for an hour break, after being locked down for twenty-three hours, he bowed on his knees and looked up as he held his arms up toward to the sun like he was praying. His mind was gone. He then got up and ran toward the fence and started climbing. The guard in the tower fired a warning shot, and he stopped, turned, and smiled and then continued climbing. He could not climb over the fence because of the razor wire, and when he finally came down off the fence, they beat his ass. He was taken to the hospital, and last I heard, they declared him insane. We never saw him again.

One prisoner told a guard he had to use the latrine, but he could not hold himself, so he peed on the floor before someone came to let him out, and he got beat for peeing on the floor. That's the way some American guards treated American prisoner in LBJ, Vietnam.

Sometimes the guards would let us out to get some sunlight. It's hot in the Hole; the tropical heat makes the cells get stuffy, and there are no fans. Because it got so hot in the daytime, nights and mornings were cold.

The racial population at the LBJ stockade was about 70 percent blacks, and other races totaled about 30 percent, I'm not being racially biased; that's the truth. The times I was in the stockade that was the population. The white guys committed severe crimes like murder. Most blacks committed crimes like going AWOL—insignificant in comparison to the crimes of the whites. Some blacks committed murder and other hard crimes, but not to the degree that the whites did.

I got out of the Hole and was returned to general population on the maximum security side. As soon as I got on the yard, I heard other prisoners talking about a riot that was in the making. This was to be my first riot. I would experience three during my entire time spent in the stockade. The riot started because the guards strip-searched and harassed us, and these guards had no experience in combat as the majority of the prisoners had. For for the guards this was their war. Many times we could not get seconds in the chow line, especially when they had fried chicken we call (barnyard pimp) on the menu. There would be enough chicken, but they would not allow prisoners seconds. You must understand: there are no food stores or hamburger stands. If the army doesn't feed you, you will not eat unless you go to the Vietnamese to eat.

Every Thursday night was movie night on the yard. They stopped the movies, and it caused frustration. The guys started walking across the yard saying, "Man, we've got to burn it down in order to show the staff they cannot treat us this way." After breakfast we returned to our bunks and waited to be called to the yard for work detail. The leaders of the riot were prisoners with rank among the other prisoners. Other prisoners listened to them and looked up to their leadership, either out of fear or respect. Prisoners passed the word around the yard that no one would fall out for work detail in protest. When the call came on the loud speaker, "Fall out for work detail," all the white prisoners went out, and the blacks stayed. I knew we were in trouble. I wanted to go with the white boys, but I knew what would happen if I went against my own even if I did not agree with them. We did not come out for formation, and the guards closed the gate to our compound. The white prisoners were taken to their work detail.

Forty riot guards came into the outer area of the compound with M-14 bayonets fixed, wearing gas masks. They formed a line across the compound. They shot us with CS gas in all three compounds. They gassed more than four hundred men. Then they opened the gate to the compounds and made us come out and get down on the ground with our hands on our heads, which was hard to do with our skin burning, eyes watering profusely, noses running like faucets; coughing, choking, gagging, and barely breathing. That was the method they used to put down the protest. I was in three riots in the stockade in Vietnam, and each time they used gas to gain control.

The leaders of the protest decided to stage the same protest the next day. That morning we were called out for work after everyone had eaten. The call went out over the loud speaker, "Fall out for formation work detail." When the white prisoners got up off their bunks, the black prisoners told them to sit down, that no one was going on work detail that day. What could they do? We were all in jail together, and blacks far outnumbered the whites, so they sat down. The call came again, and nobody moved. The guards closed the gate to our compound, and in came the riot guard like before and gassed all of us again. Usually after a riot, conditions get better. We now started getting seconds in the chow line; we got movie night back, and overall the guards treated us better because of the riot.

The only thing was that the leaders of the protest got punished. They were either put into the Box or court-martialed. The rest of us, both whites and blacks, enjoyed the fruits of their sacrifice. One morning in formation a new white prisoner was in the third row from the back. This was his first day locked up in the stockade. One of the black prisoners patted the white boy on the ass. Whenever you are incarcerated, there are prison rules on how to conduct yourself within the prison system so that you don't be taken advantage of or become someone's girl boy. He was so afraid, he turned around and smiled. I don't know if he was a homosexual or just scared. You do not allow others to take charge of your life. That evening before dark across the compound in a hooch a black prisoners had anal sex with the new prisoner—his first day on the yard. That night after everyone was in their bunks, the new prisoners got raped by ten or twelve inmates. It was not all black prisoners who took part in the rape.

One prisoner was acting as a pimp, selling the new guy to other inmates for packs of cigarettes. When the guards made their rounds outside our compound, the inmates would scatter to their beds for bed check. When the guards left, the prisoners would get him out of bed and take turns raping him again. His mannerisms upon arrival to the stockade made me believe he was a homosexual. Why didn't he tell the guard when they had bed check? He could have stopped the rape. It was sickening to see men act like dogs, each trying to be a bigger dog by outdoing the others. Another prisoner and I were watching from an adjacent tent, and it was my first time seeing men act in this manner. I had seen guys in the field enjoy the act of killing the enemy and collecting ears from dead men. But to see men rape a man made me sick to my stomach.

The scene was so disgusting, it made the other prisoner who was watching with me vomit profusely. Sex was not the focus, but men acting like animals, trying to prove who was the coldest. Wars and incarceration bring out the worst in men. The following morning the new prisoner walked across the yard to the gate and requested sick call.

That afternoon about thirty MPs stormed the compound as if they were confronting a riot situation. They gathered all the men involved in the rape of the new prisoner and took them to the Box, or solitary confinement—that place designed to drive men crazy. The rumor on the yard was that three of the guys who had raped the new guy went stone crazy in the Box. When they raped that guy it was not about sex; it was showing their power over others, how much of a man they were to other prisoners, when inside they were afraid that the same might happen to them. Some people must try to fit in to prove their power. They won't stand on their own beliefs or do what they actually believe is right. Their self-esteem is low; therefore they follow the crowd.

When there was an incident on the yard, the word spread throughout the hold compound. And when a new prisoner came on the yard, all the men in the stockade knew what he was charged with or accused of committing almost before he arrived.

I made parolee for good behavior and was sent to the other side of the stockade where living conditions were much better. There were no riots or fighting between prisoners. The food was better, and you got more of it; you could get fat on that side of the compound. Work details were also better; there were no shit-burning details. On the other side, shit details were the norm. In Vietnam, most of the armed forces' base camps had no plumbing. The toilets were outside the sleeping area. In order to get rid of the waste, we had to burn it; that's why we called it the "shit detail."

Fifty-gallon drums were cut in half and placed under the outhouses to catch waste. Inside the outhouses, which were called latrines (toilets), were long, sit-down wooden boards with approximately fifteen holes (commode seats). That was how we used the restroom. There were no stalls to have privacy while using the restroom. You sat on the commode, talking and smoking a cigarette with your neighbor while doing your business. The latrine was constructed of wood, and the back of the outhouse could be opened so that you could remove the half drum of waste to be burned. We poured gas and diesel fuel over the waste and burned it until it was consumed. This was called the "shit detail," and everyone despised this detail.

On the other side, things were different. We didn't have the white arm bands; instead we wore badges. My wife sent me a portable record player, and I had some records. There was a day room with a TV. There were no TVs on the maximum security side. We were considered model citizens on this side, and it would not be long before we were able to return to our units. In the afternoon after my work day, I cut hair in the barber shop. I cut the black prisoners' hair with a razor and comb. There were two barber chairs in that little shop.

In the corner, some of the older prisoners brewed homemade liquor in a five-gallon can. The guards never questioned the can of bubbling fruit, sugar, and yeast. The guards on this side of the compound didn't demean prisoners. When we went on a detail, we didn't have an armed guard. We had a badge showing that we were prisoners, but many times the outside people didn't know that we were prisoners, since we did not wear arm bands.

I worked for a master sergeant at Mac V headquarters, which was a large, air-conditioned building. It was modern and had three or four flights of stairs. That building housed the top brass. The master sergeant I worked for was in charge of some parts of the stockade. A female soldier who worked in his office gave me a radio, and I asked my boss if I could keep the radio. And to make sure I didn't violate the rules of the stockade, he told me he would clear me having the radio. After work I walked a mile back to the stockade with the radio and had no problem with the guard at the gate bringing the radio into the compound. The guard said, "You must know the big wheel on the hill. The radio has been cleared."

Long Binh was maybe four miles long. It had an ammunition dump, and later I was told they added a swimming pool. Most company at Long Binh were support units. On Long Binh's post there were two hospitals, the 93rd E-VAC and the 24th E-VAC, which was adjacent, about four blocks from the stockade. Mac-V headquarters was on top of the hill overlooking Long Binh. They had parades, and the guys dressed for inspection, shined their shoes, and blew bugles at formations. The atmosphere resembled stateside. There were individual homes for the big brass that lived on the base.

The master sergeant I worked for took a liking to me and pulled strings for me while I was in the stockade, and I could get away with anything. The only thing I did wrong was bring marijuana into the stockade, but I was never searched because I was referred to as the sergeant major's boy. I took advantage of his power, but pot was necessary for preserving sanity in a prison atmosphere.

Many of the other guys did the same thing. When they went out to get supplies from the replacement companies (companies that brought in goods and food), some prisoners were allowed to go on the trucks with them, and they always brought marijuana back to the stockade. Two or three trucks always returned with supplies. I never went on one of the trucks, but when they returned, there was always marijuana in the compound that night.

After I was released from the stockade, I returned to the same unit and the same company. I had been in Vietnam for fourteen months. Upon my arrival, I was told to see Major Tim before going back to the field. When I got to his office, a black E-5 greeted me and told me to sit down. Immediately I sensed that this would not be a good meeting. Major Tim leaned back in his chair. I stood at attention, eyes looking above his head as I talked to him. He asked me, "What is your problem with following orders? That was your second time in the stockade." I told him I had been wounded and returned to the field before I was completely healed, causing my wound to reopen and get infected. That started my problem. I asked him if I could put in for R&R, since I was just returning from stockade and had been In Vietnam for thirteen months with six months to complete my tour of duty. I told him I had planned to meet my wife in the Philippine for seven days.

Something I said touched a chord. He sat up in his chair and told me I was not going on R&R and that I was a yellow-bellied coward who didn't deserve to live. He told me that a man would be behind me in the field and that if we got into a firefight with the enemy and I turned to look back, that soldier had orders to shoot me in the back like a mad dog. He ordered me to return to the field the next day. A black E-5 sergeant stood beside him as he talked to me. My blood began to boil, and without thinking clearly, I leaped across the table and attacked him, I was so angry that I was in a state of shock. I reflected on the last thirteen months in Vietnam where I had been in the field, had been shot and wounded, gone AWOL, killed other men who were not my enemy, and had seen my buddies killed. I could not take the way he was talking to me, after what I have been through. I respected his position as a major, but talking to me like that caused me to lose my mind. I jumped across that desk, grabbed his throat, and tried to choke the shit out of him. I was wrong. The sergeant stopped me from killing him. I finally released him, and they removed me from the area. Major Tim kept repeating, "Get him out of here, get him out of here. Put him in stockade, put him in chains." I was put in the connex (used as a jail) with an assigned guard. I was to stay there overnight and go to the field the next day. I knew that if I went me to the field, I would be killed because I had jumped on Major Tim. Remember, I had just gotten out of jail that morning.

The guy who guarded me wanted to go to the EM Club in Phouc Vinh for a few beers. He said to me, "You're not going to run away, are you?" I answered, "Man, no. I'm not going to run." We went to the club, and he bought liquor for both of us. I poured mine out but pretended I was drinking. He got drunk and we walked back to the connex jail cell. He didn't want to lock me up, so he put me in the cell and passed out. I stayed there until almost daybreak the next morning when I broke out with my bag in hand. I walked near the gate where a guard was on duty. As I approached him, I started yelling, "Yeah, man. I've done my time. I'm going home." He actually thought I was going home. He was happy for me and didn't ask for paperwork showing that I had been released. I got past him and walked about three quarters of a mile to reach the chopper pad. I wanted to thumb a ride anywhere just to get away from my unit. Somebody said they were going to Zi An, a small place about twenty-five miles north of Saigon. I told them I needed a ride down there because I had been released to go home. The sun started rising, and my company realized I had run. They came out in jeeps looking for me. By that time, the helicopter was lifting. I was thankful they didn't radio the choppers requesting a runaway black man. I felt like a slave running from the plantation. Thank God I had gotten away.

I went to Zi An, where I caught another chopper ride to Saigon. My attitude toward the armed forces was that they could just kiss my ass. With them having treated me in such a degrading and demeaning way, damn the United States. I didn't care if I never returned. Don't take this out of context; I loved my wife, my family, and my country. They were on my mind all the time, but my life was also on the line. I was in a strange land with nowhere to turn and no one to turn to. My only thought was survival.

When I returned to Saigon, I found my buddy who was in the Air Force. I had met him while in the stockade in Long Binh. We were prison buddies. He let me stay with him. He gave me clothes to wear, and we went downtown to celebrate. He told me to forget my troubles for one night. Sure enough, we went to Soul City, Ken Hoi, the bottom part of Saigon. There were nothing but brothers there, and if you saw a white guy, a black guy had brought him there. Having been in Vietnam for thirteen months, I had given up on the idea of ever returning home.

I ran into a Cambodian prostitute who wasn't physically attractive, but I slept with her for the next three nights. That was my first sexual encounter in Vietnam and my first sexual encounter with a woman other than my wife since I had gotten married. It was just an affair, but from that experience, she became pregnant. I didn't know she was pregnant and didn't see the child until almost a year later.

I met another woman named Wau, who was a Chinese/Vietnamese prostitute. She was a very pretty woman, ten years my senior. She was part owner of the Ledo Bar where she worked. What started out as an affair gradually turned into a close relationship. I liked her a lot, and she was crazy about me and would do anything to make me happy.

I was her primary man; I never paid for sex again. Whenever I was in Saigon, I stayed at her house. She lived with her mother, who owned the housing complex where we lived. She rented the store in front of her home, which had two levels. The downstairs had a large kitchen, dining room area, bedroom, bathroom, and living room. The remaining bedrooms were upstairs. Whenever Wau had a client who stayed all night, they stayed in the downstairs bedroom. When the client fell asleep, she came upstairs and got into bed with me. I was the only client allowed upstairs, where her mother stayed.

One night while we were on the balcony talking as we enjoyed the night air and the stars, Wau said, "I love you." I asked her how could she say she loved me when she had sex with all the GIs. She reminded me that I never paid to stay at her home and that I slept upstairs where her mother slept, and she mentioned the many things she did for me without pay.

After I returned from Vietnam, my mother told me about dreams she had about a woman and me. When she awoke, she felt a sense of relief about not hearing from me. I knew the woman she dreamed of was Wau.

Wau lived in the Cholon area, a town south of Tan Son Nhut Air Force Base. There was a private, gated American swimming pool adjacent to the alley that led to her home. Everybody in the alley knew me and spoke to me when I passed through en route to Wau's house. The alley was a safe place for me. The people in that alley liked me. One day as I passed through on my way to her house, an older man at a small bar waved for me to stop. At that time, I could not speak their language well. He invited me to have a drink of rice wine with him. There was no charge for the drink. He and the other men were being friendly. The more I drank, the more I understood what they were saying to me. After a few hours I was drunk. Wau came and took me home. She helped me deal with the mental anguish of my situation. I was torn because I couldn't get back to the states. I had a wife whom I loved very much, and there I was committing adultery on foreign soil. I was also AWOL from my unit, not doing what I was sent here to do and actually a fugitive from the United States Army. I was at the lowest point of my life.

Wau helped me maintain my sanity. Her words were, "What can you do now? Can you go home? No. Can you see your wife now? No. Then deal with what you can do now and work forward to tomorrow." The wisdom she gave me helped me deal with my problems. Wau's home was the place I called home, since I had no other place to keep my personal belongings (pictures, clothes, and jewelry, including two 24-carat gold rings).

I was in downtown Saigon, and I saw a record store that sold music from the Temptations and Motown. The records were colored blue, red, and yellow, and I purchased several of these colored records. When I was put out of Vietnam, I left all my possession behind. Each time I returned to my unit, all my belongings were gone. Besides that, all the personnel I knew were dead or had gone back to the States. One day while I was at Wau's house, she told me that the next time I came home after being away for a while, she would have round eyes. I did not understand what she was telling me at that time, but when I saw her again, her eyes were black and blue, and her face was swollen. I thought to myself, *She has been an a fight*, and I was ready to find the one responsible. She said, "I told you I was going to have round eyes like the American girls." She had had plastic surgery on her eyes. About two weeks later, I saw what she was talking about. She was already a pretty Vietnamese/Chinese woman, but now she had round eyes. I was amazed at what she had done. I was a young, twenty-year-old boy from the South, and I knew nothing about plastic surgery. Needless to say, I learned a lot in Vietnam.

There was a military policeman from the Air Force who was attracted to Wau. I would see him at the Airman's Club on Tan Son Nhut Air Base, and he became one of Wau's clients/boyfriends. One night Wau brought him home to spend the night. He did not see me or know that I was upstairs. Wau had warned me about him because he was a military policeman, and I consciously avoided him on base at the club, but someone told him that I was dating his girl, Wau.

Whenever he saw me on base, he gave me the once-over look. It appeared as if he were trying to determine something about me that didn't add up; he couldn't tell if I was Army or Air Force. I became paranoid, thinking he would soon discover I was AWOL. After that I stayed out of his sight. Years later after I returned home, I tried to go back to Vietnam I became homesick for the country, and it was difficult adjusting to life in the States. I became a hippie and hitchhiked across America. This one time I was hitchhiking from home to Memphis, three members of the Black Panther Party picked me up and gave me a ride to Memphis. We made small talk, and they asked if I knew anyone in town. I said no and that I would bum around in Memphis for a while and then move on. They invited me to stay with them for a few days. We finally arrived at their headquarters. I walked in and sat with the children. There were mean-looking guys walking around in black jackets, black tams on their heads, and dark sunglasses covering their eyes.

Suddenly the door swung open, and in walked this military policeman I ran from while I was in Vietnam. What a switch from a policeman to a Black Panther! I sat on a chair with the children watching TV as those guys gave hand signs as they moved around the room. I was sure it was him. I pulled out a picture of Wau from my bag and cupped it in my hands. When he moved closer to me, I tapped him on the leg, held up Wau's picture, and asked if he knew this lady. When I tapped his leg, he sat up erect, gave me a deadly look, and said "What's up?" I had the picture in my hand. He looked down and that Negro, colored, African-American black man shouted out Wau's name. He looked at me and said, "It's you! I know you! You were in Vietnam! It's a small world." He invited me to his house, where I met his wife. He instructed me to keep silent about Wau's picture. He said his wife had found some other pictures of Wau and burned them.

I learned that war not only killed off people so that the world would not become overpopulated but that people got rich because of wars. We fought around a place called the Michelin Rubber Tree Plantation. We ran into a clearing where approximately two to three hundred rubber trees stood like solders in formation one behind the other. Those trees had buckets attached to them, and rubber dripped into the buckets. I didn't know rubber came from a tree. The trees were lined up so you could stand in front of them and step to the right or left and see clear through the end of the row of trees. You could also stand in front of a tree, and according to how you positioned yourself, you couldn't see beyond the tree in front of you.

The enemy took advantage of the tree formation and walked directly upon us before we could see them coming. I hated those damn rubber trees. Our company commander ordered us not to shoot or otherwise destroy those trees. I didn't understand the importance of the rubber tree plantation, when the enemy was using them to his advantage to attack us. After I returned to the States and saw Michelin tires on cars, I understood. I learned that American companies have some ownership in that tree plantation in Vietnam. So the question becomes, are we fighting against the spread of Communism, or are we fighting to protect special interest's profit?

Wau told me how we could make money the day before payday, but I was late getting there on that day, so she never told me that secret. On payday, the first day of the month, the color of American money changes from brown to blue. On that day, all Americans in Vietnam had to exchange all the brown paper money in order to receive the new blue paper money. One was allowed to have no more than $200 in paper money at a given time. Checks and money orders were acceptable, but not cash. If caught with a cash amount over $200, one had to give an account as to how he had gotten the money. It might have been through gambling or something other means. It was a trick.

The Vietnamese had their own paper currency. The GIs could not have the United States greenback dollar bill in Vietnam; instead, America printed the brown money to represent the American dollar bill. The American brown paper dollar was worth $2.62 in Vietnamese currency. That was pretty good. When an American GI went to town the next day after the exchange, the cab driver asked, "What is this blue note?" Well, that was the new money; the brown paper note was no good.

Some Vietnamese people had accumulated lots of brown paper money, and they committed suicide when they discovered that it was no good. My heart went out to them. They had labored long and hard for that money, now worth nothing.

One night as Wau and I were in bed talking, she drifted off to sleep. She had taught me how to meditate; it was part of her religion. She said it would help me overcome my mental state as I was learning about the world. As I mentioned earlier, Wau is ten years older than I. I was not used to her way of thinking. She taught me to focus on a dot on the wall and try not to think of anything but the dot. She was right there with me, helping to concentrate. I stared at the dot on the wall, and at first it was hard to keep my mind from wandering. But the more I practiced, the better I got. I got so I could stare at that dot and go into a trance, seeing nothing but the dot. All around the dot there appeared to be microwaves. I didn't look at the waves, just the dot. I would be in what seemed to be a hypnotic state. When I first started, Wau would bring me out of the trance. Then I started meditation on my own. I got pretty good at going into a trance and bringing myself out of the trance. That was relaxing. It calmed me down, so I didn't worry as much as I did before I started this mental exercise.

After I became experienced with meditation, I decided to try a different approach. One night after Wau drifted off to sleep, the idea came to mind to try to waken her by calling her name in my mind. She had her back toward me, so I fixed my eyes on her head. I stared at one piece of hair on her head, and I went into a trance. When I got inside her head, I called her name. I called it again and again, when suddenly she moved. I stopped calling her, and she stopped moving. I called her again. She moved; I stopped. I waited a while and started calling her again. I went in for the kill. I called until she was completely awake. She turned to me and asked, "What do you want?"

I responded with, "What are you talking about?" She said, "You keep calling me." I freaked out. What kind of stuff is this? What a power! I am a country boy from the South, and we don't do this kind of mess. What have I learned? We have so many talents and so many gifts. We don't use our minds to its full capacity—not even close.

I never tried meditation again until years later after I was home and something happened that caused me to wonder if I could still use that mental power. I had four children—two boys and two girls. One morning after church service we were on the church steps when my boys were running on the sidewalk across a one-way street with other children. Cars were parked on both sides of the street. A car was coming up the street as my son attempted to run across the street. He was getting close enough to run in front of this approaching car. I ran toward him from my side of the street and at the same time extended my hands as if I was close enough to push him out of the way. Although I was on the opposite side of the street, he fell back as if I had pushed him. My son was seven years old. He said I pushed him back as he was running toward me to cross the street. I cannot explain what happened, but it did happen. The world is too big and complex to be explained. There are some things that we will never know in this life.

I had a two-bedroom apartment in downtown Saigon. Wau was my main girlfriend, even though I had other friends. Around the corner from my apartment, Mama-san ran a house of prostitution. I don't know how old she was, but she ran the house and Papa-san was the boss. He had very little to say, but whenever he opened his mouth, people moved. Mama-san was very nice to me, and she would get on me if she thought I was smoking too much pot. She always sent a girl to sleep with me—not so much for sex but for me to have company at night. Mama-san looked out for me. I know it was also business, since she would send all the girls around to my apartment to stay the night so that the police would not see them. While the girls were there, they cooked, and we played cards and watched TV. Mama-san told me always to buy gold but not to sell it. She told me that, if you have gold, you will have money, whatever country you go to, because gold is the universal language.

One night I was sitting in the alley around the corner from my apartment relaxing and talking to friends around the food stand, People were out on their porches, and others walked up and down the alley, enjoying the weather and talking to neighbors, Vietnamese music playing on the radio. Suddenly the military police came through the alley in a military jeep. That was quite unusual; normally we were warned when the police entered the alley, but this night, there they were. It was about an hour before curfew when all GIs had to be back on base. I was the only American in the alley. I had on a silk lounge wear; I thought I was cool. The MP asked for my ID. And what was I doing in an off-limit alley?

At that time I spoke the language rather fluently. Speaking in Vietnamese, I told the girl beside me to tell the officer that I was not a black American, but a Cambodian; many Cambodians have black or dark skins and look like American blacks.

The MP said, "Damn! He looks just like a nigger." I never cracked a smile, and they moved on out of the alley. We all laughed after they left. I was AWOL from the US Army six months before I got caught. A friend that I met in the stockade was visiting some girl when the MPs came through the front door. We went out the back to the alley. I was following him and ran right into the arms of the police. I should have known better than following Tim, since I knew Saigon, whereas he didn't. They took us to jail in downtown Saigon and held us until our unit came for us. While we were there in jail, we were in a two-bunk cell facing the guard's desk. We were there for three days, and on the second day, as I sat on my bunk, the walls started to move. I asked Tim whether he had seen the walls move. He said, "The walls did not move. You're claustrophobic." He offered me a smoke to calm my nerves, and it worked; the walls stopped moving.

First Division MPs picked us up and transported us in a jeep to Di An, about twenty-five miles north of Saigon. Tim and I were both with the Big Red One Division.

I escaped into the night and stayed in Di An with some brothers I had met on another occasion. They were from the sign corps division. I did not tell them I had escaped from the police. We got high and played a bid whist card game. While I was there, seven of them planned to take a truck and go to Long Binh to see James Brown perform. They asked me to go with them, and I agreed. While living at home with my parents, I could never have gone to a show like that. I was already AWOL, so I had nothing to lose. I went with them. Those boys had not experienced combat; they were sign corps big radio operators. They worked in the bunker handling calls.

We headed twenty miles east to Long Binh on a dangerous road in one truck, with few weapons and a bag of weed. We did not know whether or not we would meet the enemy on the road; in fact, we didn't care. We were going to see James Brown, and no Viet Cong would stop us from seeing "Mr. Dynamite." We arrived there superexcited, and it was well worth the risk. Man, what a show! The place where the event took place looked like the Hollywood Bowl. James hit the stage and showed his ass. I was so glad I went. That was the only time I ever saw Bro. James live on stage.

While returning to Di An, we stopped at a bar on the side of the road. I begged the guys not to stop, but they were determined to have sex. We had no backup if something happened, and there was nobody else on the road who could offer us protection. I felt naked. I would have felt better if I had been alone, but there were seven guys and five M-16s and no additional ammunition. Well, there was nothing I could do but brace myself for whatever happened. I did not want to have sex with those little hot-tail girls who probably had VC for boyfriends.

Mama-san asked whether I wanted to have sex with one of the young girls. I replied, "No! I want to have sex with you, Mama-san." She said, "No, me Mama-san." I was content and waited for the guys. Clearly, it wasn't that I didn't want to have sex; I didn't want to catch the claps or get gonorrhea. Mama-san was forty-four years old and my best chance of not getting a disease. A few minutes later Mama-san came back and said, "Me can do." I had sex with her.

I was twenty at the time, and to this day I think of Mama-san.

Out of three years of having sex with Vietnamese girls, I only caught gonorrhea one time, and that was from my main lady, Wau. I thank God for His protection, especially when I think of the AIDS virus.

We returned safely to Di An, and the following morning I got a chopper back to Saigon where I lived another six months. I never saw Tim again. Back home in Saigon I resumed my life as a fugitive. Dealing in the black market, I met a man called Mr. China-man. He was Chinese, and I believe he was a top man in the Chinese mafia. After we established a trusting relationship, and he learned I was AWOL, he set me up where I made money through him on the black market. After I had worked with him for a while, he offered me a way to get to America with official-looking papers that replicated the Army's and a first-class plane ticket back to the States without the Army's knowledge. I found out that the MPs in the States did go to my mother's and wife's houses looking for me and had mistaken my brother, who lived in New York and was visiting my mother's house, for me, while I was in AWOL in Vietnam. He had to show his ID before they believed him.

I thanked Mr. China-man but told him that was not the way I wanted to go back, that I would get home on my own, and if I never made it back to the United States, then Saigon would be my home. Forgery was something the Vietnamese did well. They would take marijuana and package it like an unopened carton of cigarettes, and the only way you could tell the difference was that the end of the cigarette would be folded. The carton of marijuana cigarettes would have the government seal as if it had never been opened.

I met VC who came to Saigon to visit families and friends at the Vietnamese New Year (Tet). I talked politics with Vietnamese people living in my apartment building. After living in Saigon for one year, I returned to my unit. They had moved from Phouc Vhin to Quan Loi. Before I left Saigon, Mama-san begged me to stay, but when she saw that my mind was made up, she told me not to travel by road. I told her I was going to fly. That was the last time I saw Mama-san. When I arrived at Quan Loi, the unit was sitting on a red dirt hill. It was the dry season, and when you walked, your feet would sink into silky, soft, red dirt. I had never seen soil like that before. Everything was red—the tents and the grass on the side of the road. In the rainy season the red dirt turned to slick mud, and even the palms of your hands were red. I walked into the orderly room (front office) and announced that I was Robert Rice. At first they thought I was a new arrival fresh from the States, but after they heard my name someone said, "Get him." The company commander came from out of his office, greeted me, and said, "Welcome back. I've heard a lot about you." Immediately two soldiers were assigned to guard me. After three weeks I was given a special court-martial and found guilty, and I received the maximum sentence of six months.

When I arrived at LBJ, I was recognized by one of the guards as an old-timer who had been there before and had returned home to jail. I don't know of anyone who served as much time at LBJ as I did. Instantly, that gave me credibility with other prisoners on the compound. That meant I did not have to fight for rank within the prison system. My status as a prisoner had been upgraded. I got respect based on being an "old-timer."

In the field there were snakes, bugs, ants, blood suckers, and many other creatures that would eat you. But I had never been eaten alive until I went back to the stockade and caught the crabs from sitting on the toilets. I itched wherever there was hair, and I am quite hairy. I was taking a shower when one of the crabs and his family asked me for soap (just a joke). I was infested with them. The medic gave me some blue ointment to put all over the hairy parts of my body. I walked/slid around the yard for three days with this blue stuff on me. It felt like grease on my body. But I never had crabs again.

I met a guy named Smith who was from my hometown. I remembered seeing him when I was about ten years old. We never associated with one another then. When I saw Smith in the stockade, I said, "Man, I remember you from Chattanooga." He didn't remember me, but we knew some of the same people, and because of that hometown connection we became close and depended on each other for protection. After I left the stockade, I never saw Smith again. I looked for him after I returned to Chattanooga, but nobody knew anything about him. I left Vietnam in 1969, and in 2000 I became a licensed minister of the gospel Jesus Christ and minister at the local prison in Chattanooga. I conduct service every Wednesday night for about two hours, and one night while I was speaking to roughly thirty-five inmates, one of them caused me to stop abruptly. The others were wondering what was wrong. I said to this inmate who caught my eye, "Do you know anyone named Smith?" He said, "That's my daddy you are talking about." I was elated that I had finally found my buddy, Smith. I asked about his father and he said, "He died when I was two years old." That was a heartbreaking and disappointing moment. He told me that his father had been killed in a shootout. He didn't remember his father, but everyone said he looked just like him, which is why I stopped preaching—because he looked just like his daddy. Well, from that day he was like my own son, and he felt the same about me; he had found someone who had known his father. I like to think I may have made a difference in his life through the preaching of Jesus Christ. He was back and forth, in and out of jail, and constantly in trouble with the law. His family was tired of bailing him out of trouble. The last time I saw him on the outside was on a local TV church program. He was in the front row of the church. Tears flowed down my face; it me made so happy to see him in church on the outside and not on the inside of a jailhouse church.

One day after work detail I was told to report to the major's office. I was shocked, not knowing what it was about. In his office he had me sit down, and he told me he was going to put me in the Box. I asked, "What have I done?" That's when he handed me a letter and said, "Read this." The letter opened by saying, "Dear Robert." We called these types of letters "Dear John letters," meaning, "It's over. I found someone else." When your woman quits you, it is a hurting thing, but when she quits you while you are incarcerated and in Vietnam, it's worse. I had been in Vietnam for more than two years and had not been home. One of my homeboys went back home and told my wife that he had run into me and that I was addicted to drugs and was living in a whorehouse, pimping women, and would never come back to America. He was trying to have sex with my wife, she told me years later. In the letter she included divorce papers.

At the bottom of the paper she wrote, "If you still love me, don't sign these papers." For me that meant she still loved me but was confused about my situation.

She didn't know why I was not home or why I had not written her. Her letter gave me hope that our marriage could still be salvaged. I convinced the major that I was not going to try to escape. So I didn't go to the Hole. I went back to my bunk. I heard some of the fellows singing and playing drums on gallon cans, and it sounded like a radio playing. I put that letter away and went over to their tent and got high. I never signed those divorce papers. One of my work details included running a large washing machine for the 24th E-VAC hospital, which was located about one half mile down the road from the stockade. One day, after catching up on my washing duties, I was walking on the ward, and there I saw an old classmate. We had grown up in the same community and were in first grade together. I knew him very well. We made eye contact, and at the same time called each other by name.

He said, "They got me, Robert Lee." All my childhood friends called me by that name. I asked, "What the hell happened to you?" and he told how he was hit by a booby-trap bomb the enemy had set. It exploded and hit him. He was bandaged from one arm, around his side and back, as well as his leg.

I told him I was in the stockade and was assigned to work at the hospital. He was surprised and amazed because I had never been one to get in trouble. He said, "Robert Lee, you never got into trouble at home." I told him I knew.

The next time I saw him, we were home on the streets, and he always said how glad he had been to see me so far from Chattanooga.

While I was lying on my bunk reading in the stockade, the sky suddenly turned red, and a few seconds later, there was a loud boom. The power and the sound of the blast knocked me off my bunk. The siren went off, warning that the base was under attack.

That was the start of the Vietnamese New Year (the Tet Offensive). Tet is like our New Year, but this year the enemy hit many US military bases in Vietnam simultaneously. The VC hit the ammunition dump, which was less than a mile away from the stockade. They blew it up, and the ammunition dump exploded for the next five days and nights. Every few minutes a round went off, and we were in constant fear of one of the rounds hitting us in the stockade. The ammo dump should have been buried underground instead of being stacked on top of the ground. It had the capacity to supply Long Binh, one of the largest US Army facilities in Vietnam, which had a population of 60,000. I was released from the stockade for the third time. That was in the midst of the ammo dump blasting. I was instructed to return to my unit, but instead I went home to Saigon to Wau's house. I walked about a mile to the main gate of Long Binh, and off the base I got on Highway One and hitchhiked a ride in a small Vietnamese vehicle to Saigon. When I look back, I think I had to be crazy to do all those things.

On the way to Saigon, Papa-san warned me there were VC everywhere. When I arrived in Saigon, the streets were deserted. There were very few people moving around— walking or riding. Anyone seen on the streets was moving swiftly. I had never seen Saigon like this; people peeped through windows at movement on the streets. They were afraid to come outside. When I approached the alley that led to Wau's house, it was empty. I reached her house and knocked on the door, but she did not open it. Instead, she answered through the door. After I identified myself, she peeped out to be sure. Then she slowly opened the door and pulled me inside. I could see the fear in her face. She said, "You are crazy! The VC are everywhere. How did you get here?" That same night, on the balcony off the bedroom, we saw the VC moving in the moonlight through the graveyard toward Tan Son Nhut Air Base. I felt naked. If they had come to the house, I would have been on my own. I had nothing with which to defend myself. After a week or more, Saigon returned to normalcy.

I stayed in Saigon long enough to be considered AWOL. When I return to my unit, they had moved again. This time First Division Black Lion had moved to Lai Khe.

I arrived late by a few months and again was court-martialed and sentenced to six months confinement in the stockade. This time General Westmoreland said, "If any GI had six months or less, he will only be confined for one month." Where was he in 1966 when I first went to the stockade? I spent a total of fifteen and a half months in the stockade. Each time I was court-martialed, I was returned to my same company B. According to the UMCJ, a book of army laws, I should have been put in a different company each time I returned from the stockade, but that did not happen. I returned to my unit and was told to report to the major general's office. He said I would be going home, but with a bad conduct discharge. I wouldn't have any rights under the GI Bill. He presented some papers for me to sign, showing my agreement with the discharge. I thought about the blood I spilled on the battlefield and all the shit I'd been through, and there was no way in hell I would sign that discharge. If I had signed, I would have been on my way home, but I refused to sign the paper. The major said that, if I wanted to go home, I had to sign, and again I told him I was not going to sign and that I was already at home. I had been in Vietnam so long, it felt like home, and I was content staying there. To be honest, I was afraid to go back to America. The major was mad as hell at me. He demanded that I leave his office, and as I was leaving, he shouted, "Your ass will never go home." I shouted, "I'm already at home."

I returned to my company and was under the leadership of a very empathetic first sergeant. He ask me how long had I been in Vietnam. I told him I was in my third year He proposed a plan that would get me some good time toward my tour of duty so I could return to the States. He had me work three or four nights a week in the command bunker manning the radio for the perimeter, and he covered me on my days off. He wasn't concerned about what I did or where I went, as long as I reported on the scheduled work days. I agreed, and we shook hands. I took my orders from him, and the company commander had nothing to do with me; he was true to his word. On my off days I was on my own. No other officers gave me orders to do anything. On my off days I went home to Saigon. My life was going well, and I was finally back on the right track. I could have lived like that for years, but one day I had completed a night shift and gotten into bed when two soldiers came into my tent. One was a second lieutenant, and the other was an E-6, who said, "Robert Rice, you have been discharged, and you are going home." You would think that this would have been the happiest day of my life, but it wasn't. I protested, saying, "Get out of my tent." He said, "Man, you're going home." I then asked, "What type of discharge?" and he said, "212, under honorable conditions." I was in shock. I didn't want to go back to America, where I had no wife, no hope, and an uncertain welcome. I had planned to accept the discharge and go home to Saigon and think things over, but the two soldiers said that they would stay and escort me to clear post. They accompanied me for the next three days, not letting me out of their sight, all the way to the steps of the airplane to make sure I left Vietnam. If they had not been with me those three days, I would never have made it back to the United States. I was too scared to come home. I had been scared to go to Vietnam and was now scared to leave. When the airplane lifted and banked over Saigon, tears flooded down my face. Other soldiers were cheering, but not me. I didn't have a chance to say good-bye to Wau or my other Vietnamese friends or my son, whom I would never see again. It was an extremely sad time.

It's now 2014, and at last I'm finishing this book. It has taken me over twenty years to write, starting and stopping, yet I still feel sad about leaving Saigon. I have learned that in this life, nothing stays the same; people come into your life, and they leave, and the only thing that lasts is precious memories.

I arrived in the United States on January 20, 1969, to a physically cold world; it was forty degrees. When I got home, there were no big guns going off. It was very quiet, and I almost had a mental breakdown trying to adjust to the quietness. My marriage was over, and I seemed to be all alone. My family was happy to see me, but things had changed; it wasn't the same. The first year back home trying to adjust was very difficult. My father got me a job at his place of employment, and I eventually remarried, and my wife and I had four children. I enrolled in night school and received my high school diploma.

For the next sixteen years I tried to make my marriage to my second wife work, but Vietnam was still in my head, and after exhausting every effort, we divorced. I ran into my first wife at the store, and our marriages to others hadn't worked out, so we reunited.

I entered a therapy program at the Veteran's Administration that helped veterans deal with combat stress syndrome. A combat-wounded veteran counselor encouraged me to write this book. He said he had heard many stories from veterans, but my story surpassed them all. His words gave me insight as to why it was so hard for me to adjust to life outside Vietnam. I went on to college and to seminary school and became a licensed minister focusing on prison ministry, since I certainly had a lot of experience in that field.

When I told you about the angel I saw on the battlefield, as I lay there trying to die, asking me about my first wife and giving me a reason to live, I believe the angel knew the future, whereas we mortals don't understand the unseen world. My life has been one big adventure that God the Father knows all about. I am thankful to God the Father and His Son, the Lord Jesus Christ, who have kept and carried me along for this ride of life.

I am hopeful that my story will allow you, the reader, to see what many soldiers have to endure, regardless of the war. God is in control. He says in His Word:

> *And we know that all things work together for good to them that love God, to them who are called according to his purpose* (Rom. 8:28).

About the Author

Robert L. Rice completed high school after completing his tour of duty with the United States Army. He later graduated from Covington School of Theology. He is currently serving as an associate minister at the Orchard Knob Missionary Baptist Church in Chattanooga, Tennessee. He also heads the prison ministry at Silverdale Correctional Facility under the authority of Orchard Knob Missionary Baptist Church. His experiences in the United States military equipped him with the tools necessary to minister to inmates.

Printed in the United States
By Bookmasters